M000117094

 Unit 5
Decodable Reader

Mc
Graw
Hill
Education

Bothell, WA • Chicago, IL • Columbus, OH • New York, NY

Contents

by Albert Santiago
illustrated by Kate Flanagan

17

Pam and Tam

by Claire Bradley

illustrated by Olivia Cole

Tam can  to Pam.

wave

Pam can tap on the cap.
Pam can pat it on.

The cap sat on top.
Do you see it?

The cap can **go**!
Can Tam nip it?

Tam did nip it!

Tam can pat, pat, pat it on.
Tam can **go**.

Sid Can Hop

by Celine Robbins

A  can sit.

dog

It can sit, sit, sit.

A bat can nap.
It can nap, nap, nap.

A cat can tip it.
It can tip, tip, tip it.

A  bird can tap.

It can tap, tap, tap.

Photo: Cappi Thompson/Flickr/Getty Images; Art: Geoffrey Smith

My tan  can hop.
rabbit

See him hop, hop, hop.

15

I like **my** Sid!

My Pet Ed

by Albert Santiago

illustrated by Kate Flanagan

I am Ted.
I like  .
dogs

Mom set Ed on .
grass
Ted met Ed.

20

Ted ran.
Ed ran.

Ed ran, ran, ran.
Ted ran, ran, ran.

Ted and Ed sat on a .

bike

Ted can pet Ed.
Ted and Ed **are**  !

24

friends

Unit 5

Decodable Words
Target Phonics Elements: Review Short *i;*
Initial /*n*/*n;* Initial /*k*/*c;* Short *o;*
Initial and Final /*d*/*d*
can, cap, did, it, nip, not, on, tip, top
Review: *Pam, pat, Tam, sat*

High-Frequency Words
and, do, go, to, you
Review: *see, the*

Decodable Words
Target Phonics Element: Consonant /*h*/*h*
him, hop
Review: *bat, can, cat, it, nap, Sid, sit, tan, tap, tip*

High-Frequency Words
my
Review: *a, I, like, see*

Week 3 • *My Pet Ed*

Word Count: 41

Decodable Words
Target Phonics Element: Short *e*
Ed, met, pet, set, Ted
Review: *am, can, Mom, on, ran, sat*

High-Frequency Words
are
Review: *a, and, I, like, my*

Decoding skills taught to date:

Consonants /m/*m*, /s/*s*, /p/*p*, /t/*t*; Short *a*; Short *i*; Initial and Final /n/*n*; Initial /k/*c*; Short *o*; Initial and Final /d/*d*; Consonant /h/*h*; Short *e*